Also by Myung Mi Kim

Commons, University of California Press, 2002

DURA, Sun & Moon, 1999

The Bounty, Chax Press, 1996

Under Flag, Kelsey Street Press, 1991

Penury

Penury

Myung Mi Kim

OMNIDAWN
RICHMOND, CALIFORNIA
2009

Cover art by John Fraser: "Two Squares,"
Graphite, Acrylic, Mixed Media Collage, on Wood
Construction, 13.625" x 9.375" x 1" (2007).
Courtesy of Roy Boyd Gallery, Chicago, Ill.
(www.royboydgallery.com).

Printed in the United States

by Books International, Dulles, Virginia

Cover and Interior Design by Ken Keegan

Library of Congress Catalog-in-Publication Data

Kim, Myung Mi, 1957–
    Penury / Myung Mi Kim.
        p. cm.
    ISBN 978-1-890650-37-7 (pbk. : acid-free paper)
    I. Title.
    PS3561.I414P46 2009
    811'.54--dc22

                                        2009015633

Published by Omnidawn Publishing, Richmond, California
www.omnidawn.com   (510) 237-5472   (800) 792-4957

                10 9 8 7 6 5 4 3 2

            ISBN: 978-1-890650-37-7

Grateful acknowledgment to *Conjunctions*, *XCP: Cross-cultural Poetics*, *boundary 2*, and *big bridge* where versions of some of these poems first appeared. A version of "Fell" was published by belladonna books. Thanks also to Atticus/Finch Chapbooks for publishing excerpts from *Penury* in *River Antes*.

· · ·

Increased chatter

My Booke and Filial

Reserved for pronounced sounds

To carry, more (at) to bear

Stave

For which no pronunciation exists

tw   neither bird nor ornament

the calf stranded across the creek | that bellowing

the ragged ranges

as by
one's ears

staum | *stam*

the makeshift shelter's direct proportion of drinking water to raw sewage

asperline | *tharp*

: just a normal customer with no heavy accent at all

minimum human subsistence experiment

deemed not worthy of destroying   .   public order   .   kneeling

on the ground   .   hastily dug   .   ditches, syringes   .   hoarding   .

withholding   .   designed to starve the whole region into submission

: the place I'm from is no longer on any map

‖ salute

to brethren | red

wash

ret ‖

clear burn

the entire vertical profile . from atmosphere to subsurface . columns

and processions . mustard seed . incendiary aphid . of being in

and affecting . I don't know what's the problems in that family .

probably poorness

Scn:
Scn:
Scn: Those 840 workers? They're just gone—

[offering to general protectors]

why is it that the tips of the beaks are burnt

[behest]

freedom of residence

freedom of movement

as history knows

what justice looks like

industry's station

street by street

smelting is in progress

and the rejoicing

Scn: Kwik-Pik

Scn:

Scn: send home money every four months

[lookout   post]

Are these your names

From   we are from   where are you from

Say this may speaking

To burn or expose to the threat of the sun a person
with a pigeon chest and protruding stomach

valley covered men ant size carry out

largest rat ever dugout mountain pass we took

line map anything moving marshal stomp

tons millions plastic skin fused

infrared instinctively felt for

rushed worthy arterial many friends

aggression anywhere precision elite

command record commemoration meal

At the quarry

Leaving the Quarry

Bringing hand tools

Approaching the river

The workmen are prisoners

A chariot is pulled by two servants

At the left heads are counted and the booty is piled in front of clerks
who are recording the details in a book and on a scroll

Tablet VI Panel 53

foundry
mill
warehouse

tannery
refinery
central clearing hall

infirmary
barracks
internment camp

auto plant
containment center
refugee camp

.

Touching Reception and

Precedence, the Treatment of Audience

Contents of Visiting
Ambassadors

The bird for prosperity we provided you

[conjugate]

she, the weeping work

parade of earnings

      || weight of forelegs and hooves under water

a ripple | birched

alyssum

within a few years it learns to read—if it is a boy—and in this place

the catalogue of books may be inserted

Half a lobe and barricade | as befits a stateroom

Clock-tower and bulwark

: Why don't you take mommy swimming? It'll be fun—

      He is not making rent.
      She is tired of being alone with the child.

plethora of roots || mowed lawns

tendon and refuse, who

cowered | supermarkets, windshield

snap. Does the single tree

list. Disinterred. Would be forced to look.

[conjugate]

A dependent's call

A dependent cries out

A || marvel perceive

Through sameness of language is produced

sameness of sentiment and thought

: Got up to cut meat

   Stood in that smell all day

beat/th/rone

beat/hrone

bea/t/rone

perimeter onset plain crucial corridor

branch full tip time and place

scanned yes sir I do three of those were

fixing it no seeing them elements buffer

in that twitch feel of limbs there's no fixing it

huddle quadrant counting inhabitants

operative swath who is in there who's there blaring

rout will be returned as practicable as possible

mp
lm
ks
nc
lk
lp
nh
gy
td
nc

you speak English so well transcript

∴

I go to my father's house

I wear a grief hat

I am told to put on coarse hemp and to proceed on my own

Calling of name sound, turned

Pick at   root out

An old tailor   needle ear threading   keeping eyes on us

Could the rock be that yellow, canary yellow

Corresponding

Pelvis Bowl

Bunker buster bomb

expert shores toppling hunt

continue hunt Bull Dog help hunt

claim vital time and place prohibit

shield slipped first wave accelerate

swarming hand-held toll scrutinize

green color on the face control

wear down tamp take away choice

heavy knotted free flash skyward

ones under murder coats . blue line green loop of adherence . this

is the designated pick up spot . a log buttressed the entry . demand

of numbers . derricks . daughters and sons . that announced click .

with which . to wait for the person who has left . a pump

turning itself on

.

[_____ years and _____ months]

Restored

Crossed

Led

Captured

Struck

Confronted

Launched

Removed

Spread

Stabilized

Mold attacks ears and nose

The meaning may be do not entreat

Familiar face grasped

Looking close   a stranger

you are now leaving the American sector . Perpetual Savings and Loan .

drudgery of use . shamblefall . under an obligation or necessity .

when the fish die all at once and appear on the banks all at once

[tending   quell]

if the clock were at an angle . consistent with the height

of the child . the lunch lady is walking down the drive so we know

we are late . flower boxes mistaken antidote . shrubbery money .

vacant boarded . steps of the courthouse . grateful that one pan is clean

and cooking can begin . seen nothing but the insides of things .

forlorn me in my house | forlorn you in yours

accumulation of land	maintain household bear	labor of house child
cooking reserve line	belonging to	elaborate isolation
familias implements	enemies captured in war	bearing child rearing
production heirs number	and rear household	family contains
counting herds possessions	fellow feeling crude	isolate care
family contains in germ	bearing rearing	accumulation of land
implements of production	cooking reserve line of	the number belonging
counting possessions	heirs	the captured
isolated	household bear	rear heirs
feeling crude	belonging to	fellow feeling crude

[ruins   library]

where the route of a ship bringing tax grain from the provinces is described

where perceived hindering—say, birds congregating on a runway

where the first request was for fertilizer and seeds

where the instruction—harness these to the benefit of your society

where the conscription continued

where boards of revenue

where basically, everyone had a plant job

where preventable diseases rampant

where the need is window screens and sewer covers

where for the good of the very few and the suffering of a great many

:::

fell

(for six mutlilingual voices)

: | Measure streets by the number of uniforms

: | It's the pitch of the cry that carries

: | Hunger noise thirst noise fear noise

: | Inside acts conducted outside

: | Decades of continuous drought

: | Weapon and deed

: | Whether the house has windows, whether the windows have glass

: | The dirt air

: | Of the tens of thousands of women who leave each year

: | Electric baton   rifle butts

: | Fifty cents more and we go there

: | Calculated withholding of food

maim trough

||

goods have mutual fit martial hand

||

heady courtesy

: | The epidemic phase of famine

: | Sea surface temperature   urban heat island

: | Stripped bark from pines and boiled it—and swallowed it

: | Housemaids elsewhere

: | Sacrifices to the Altar of Land and Grain

: | Foreign Employment Bureau

: | Two six seven years and my sons grown

: | Strike point   full force

: | Border security operation

: | When you come, you start from the scratch

: | Do you have guns drugs or needles in the car?

: | Do you have guns drugs or needles in the car?

Water without water third day wait

Yelling the dawn beautiful deafening

Step on people with shoes on

: | Press this button, no dust

: | Do you understand—walls surround you

: | Blowout fracture

: | That hand   placed on

·

: | Ensconced so that only the gate is visible and nothing beyond

: | Famine carried out of meteorological bounds

: | Tree   frog   toads

: | I send them candy wrapped in socks

: | The extent of the land that must be cleared for tank traffic

: | Boulders hang from my shoulders

: | Scorched earth tactics

: | Nights spent askew in a cauldron

That which is forced outside flesh

Cloven tourniquet

Draped in the last affection

:::

[Reader of the Announcement of the Spirit]

Place in the nose a piece of blue paper

The hair is combed and parted in the middle

Any fallen hair is collected and put in a pouch

With a spoon carved from a willow tree

Place three spoonfuls of rice in the mouth

Seven times bound with rope

supplar is not a word   mustard yellow is

said the master the student said the bumbling ones

sentries

mining to powder

seedling to motes

torches held at uniform height . everyone and everything seems .

whit . flaw beat . position of the storage jars . tuning fork .

onto itself . sentence stress sentence trees . guttural

The said release   annexed   surrendered

Majority of members

In consideration of lawful money

The said water frontage and the above described lands

Rolling country   small poplar bluffs

One Arrow transcript

arri

        sway

avri

someone teaches | "topic sentence"

allegiance garland

air split east up direct no grudge

pinpoint recognize wallet sized card

alert ask questions look all around

intervals flank roadside sequence

containment notch provisions means

rotors disintegrate stone compel

sand coil hard choices

strange fetch offices blistered lull

In attendance on (a person)

: Don't lie, don't say retrievable—shipped each tagged and marked

obverse view k

nitrogen oxides, heavy metal (mercury) deposits

not people—dogs, lowly animals—we were taught

the dead framed in black cardboard

obverse view t

sacrifices to those who have died in epidemics

the demand for young slender women

she thought she heard the photos

from the ones cutting

e-e   ea   ee   o-e   oa

: native speakers, the acoustic cues they expect
   (cues for native listeners come from native speakers)

allophones and alternations
sonorant
strident
nasal
anterior
coronal

a smelt in the bell | vellum

fern spread   gull flung

They must be taught the language which they must use in transacting
business with the people of this country

sm (u) n

(~)

Do you eat berries, mushrooms, fish, and game?
Most likely how it entered your body.

Place fruit of red colors to the east

Place fruit of white colors to the west

Go to the roof and call out the name

Garb   willow

To desire to see the corpse again

The father led the twigs

Bent at the waist nose nearly touching ground

Trolling sense

wicked rounding swept cliff || burial mound numb dispense

guarded ravine hoarse hail || pilfer citizen reedy gibber

|| mendacity one head four faces

stinging nettles

wild scythe swing

machines hunch

vehicles in and out

spar wanton drear dear forbid || rest cleft hold avarice swift

regard ally press fray reason || rights tie wallow heaving cause

hold facing simple adore one ||

To construct the hundred and two sections of the *Porphemes of the Rude*

Tiger in the grease barrel begins :

One night the calcified hand and arrow branded throat bound by green
sticks consoled leafy fistfuls of salt where the mends were,
at about the height of a scrawny two year old

Baleful Ladies of the Five Directions speak :

The dead have no navels

sleep chores mar

open night's scrap

Abode, braver, avow

Rat teeth clemency

The rubble in comfort

flur   also   *thist*

waste populace

infirm slants

tedious gnash || thicket lope

welt flee armor

lung sheaf

wood or its texture   .   bridge   .   standing on it or near it

imprision   it tastes of granite and the rapids

This is the isthmus of *set veron ste baro* pounded by the tides of oceans

River's fray

With head bowed walked trudged

Iron leaf once trumpets

Humpspine blackened with flies

hooded   fortune   snare   willful   wield

|

hummock   pled   sweet   water   mottled

|

abrupt   bundle   specular   scruple   prone

Fighting house by house

You saw it and you heard it?

Grass grew from the sternum

Roots took over the mandible

Near One, do you recall Day Ceremony

celebrated by a family for the welfare of all belonging to it

at the appointed time all work ceases

instruments of labor lie untouched

chants, though their precise meaning was long since become unintelligible

recited from a scroll

kept in the painted chest in the hall

sumptuous blossoms and green herbs thrown into the fire

fresh gathered from a particular plot in the garden, set apart for this purpose light of the full poor cell

verdant meeting duty is

With the head of happiness

Comfortably full of air

Abdomen boat

O hewn

cherich apere

bliss and tenderage

kind property brew speech rose

such errant rapt

refection, attend

leun   lubon

errant rapt refraction

kind speech bliss

flur also thist

beris beryl barris rose

When the book opens and the dead march

barrow flower

bulldozed | sun

Radiant falcon
Scattering acacias

The recitation of acacias
A grove of riverbeds

Residence of years' repose
Patience aids such

A bank of wide hands
Tender petition

Horizon slope, a hoop(ed) light
A fragrant sight beheld beholds

Where in this, further dwelt
Abide

Nestled close
Civil bound

Myung Mi Kim is a Professor of English and a core faculty member of the Poetics Program at the State University of New York at Buffalo. Kim has also served as Distinguished Visiting Poet at Saint Mary's College, Moraga, California, and as Visiting Professor at Oberlin College. Kim was awarded The Multicultural Publisher's Exchange Award of Merit for *Under Flag* (Kelsey Street Press, 1991). She also received a fellowship from the Djerassi Resident Artists Program, awards from the Fund for Poetry, a Daesan Foundation Translation Grant, and the State University of New York Chancellor's Award for Excellence in Scholarship and Creative Activity.